Loyal Love:
Learning the Art of
Unconditional Self-Respect

Written by
Kristi Bowman Morgan

Cover design by
Gabrielle Miranda

ISBN: 978-1-0919-1266-3

DEDICATION

For the beautiful souls who have quietly doubted their self-worth, let someone else define their happiness or ignored their gut instincts, these daily encouragements are for you.

Let every page of this inspirational guide meet you on your journey of loyal love.

From the first paragraph to the last, always remember: you are more than enough – just the way you are.

❧ Loyal Love ❧

FORWARD

For this inspirational writer, lifelong learner and passionate communicator, my *Learning the Art of Unconditional* trilogy would not be fully complete without writing about the most challenging life lesson of all: unconditional self-respect.

Self-respect does not happen overnight.   It is often built, layer by layer, tear by tear, smile by smile, from the lessons of our journey. Through both our failed relationships and our successful ones, we learn, grow and adjust our steps as we go.

As you listen to your small, steady voice, this book of reminders will help you understand the beauty of loyal love – and fully accept yourself for exactly who you are.

If you haven't written a short note to your past, I'll get us started. Let's leave yesterday behind us and move forward.

Together, let's embrace the journey to *Loyal Love: Learning the Art of Unconditional Self-Respect.*

Dear younger you,

You are worth so much more than what the world may think of you. You are stronger than your first broken heart. You are humbler than your greatest success. You are wiser than the sum of all your mistakes.

You are not less valuable because of a fluctuating number on the scale or the size of your clothes. Your opinions matter because you matter.

Through the journey of letting go and moving forward, we'll walk, arm in arm, to the path to self-respect – one beautiful step at a time.

You are LOYAL LOVE.

⌇

⁂

❞ Loyal Love ❝

WHY HELLO THERE

Have you ever had a friend you could be brutally honest with? Consider me that friend for the next hundred and thirty pages or so.

And like most loyal, but true friends, I promise you this:

I'm not going to sugarcoat it.

The pages of this book are designed to challenge you. Somewhere along the way - while trying to be all things to all people and raise kids and have a job and go to school and plan dinner and pick up the mail - you forgot the importance of respecting yourself.

It's okay.

I get it.

I've been there - done that.

And this is how and why this book had to be written. From and through and by my own experiences, I want to teach you how to fiercely and loyally love yourself, no matter what.

In hindsight, some of the most foolish choices I have ever made were because I lacked unconditional self -respect. But no more.

Now, I'm all about teaching others how to master the art that teaches the most important love of all - how to honestly and loyally love who you are – as you are – on the good days and bad days and everything in between.

Let's get started.

INVEST IN YOU

If we spend thousands of dollars on gifts for other people around the holidays, birthdays or other celebrations, why don't we make the same investment in ourselves?

What stops us from spending the money we earn on our own mental, spiritually and emotional health? What tells us we are not worthy of that investment?

Loyal Love will teach you learning to love yourself is worth way more than a monetary investment.

Loyal Love is about more than the investment of time. It's about the investment of positive affirmation.

It's about the investment of believing that you matter.

If there have been people along your journey who didn't treat you the way you deserve to be treated, this book is for you.

If you have struggled with a positive self-image and felt like giving up, read on.

Through these daily affirmations, you will not only begin to find and recognize the journey to self-worth, but you'll gracefully and humbly accept the very qualities about yourself that make you - YOU.

GIVE YOURSELF PERMISSION

Do you ever have days when you don't want to adult anymore?

I know I have. And that's ok.

Have you somehow created the illusion someone needs to permit you to follow your dreams or heaven forbid – take time just for you?

Did you know the only person who will understand the deep recesses of your heart is the same person staring back at you in the mirror?

If you are too wrapped up in what 'everyone' thinks you should be doing or not doing - take heart. It's not too late to begin again.

Give yourself permission to get to know yourself. Stop racing towards the finish line and find peace in the offering. Take a deep breath, embrace the good as well as the bad and let go of what you can't control.

The first step to loving who you are and how you are in this **Loyal Love** journey starts now.

Sign your permission slip to self-confidence in pen, not pencil. Stop erasing the versions of yourself which can only be found in fairy tales or through Photoshop.

Just. Be. You.

WHEN ONE DOOR CLOSES

Rejection isn't a failure, but a precursor to your future success.

The job you didn't get. The college that said 'thanks, but no thanks'. The cute boy you asked to the Sadie Hawkins dance who inexplicably turned you down. The feeling you had after being chosen last when the dodgeball teams were being formed.

When your heart is hurting, sometimes it is difficult to understand the why behind the what. But take heart, all is not lost.

Sometimes when one door closes, God is simply protecting you from the worst and preparing you for the best.

Does it feel good to hear the word 'NO'? Of course not.

But someday - when you look back on your life - you will see the beautiful light that was shining under the closed doors and how it was gently leading you to the path you were supposed to be on the whole time.

So take heart. Long-lasting and loyal love is found in every door that has closed.

You just need to trust the closed doors long after they have shut.

NUMBERS OBSESSED

We've all done it.

Gotten on the scale to see how much 'progress' we made over the week in reaching our goal weight. Checked the stats of our favorite MLB pitcher only to comment he must have had an 'off' game if he only struck out three but walked four.

Compared our kid's SAT scores to our friends. Gone back to a post only to check the number of "likes." Focused on what place our team came in. Lost confidence in our bodies because of our BMI.

And on it goes. There are endless numbers and calculations that are a feeble attempt to measure true excellence.

But what the measurements don't tell you are the hopes, dreams and passions of the person on the other side of the metrics. Their struggles. Their challenges. Their need for inclusion or acceptance.

Self-confidence is a lifelong process.

In the simplest of terms, it's the act of ignoring the numbers - of somehow releasing ourselves from what society says is "good" or "great."

It's about separating our hearts from blanket analysis that only tells one part of a situation.

Stop obsessing and start living. The weight of the world will lift from your shoulders the moment that you do.

HEART MOMENTS

Every day we are given endless opportunities.

We can choose to listen. We can find the rhythm of unconditional love. We can surpass all logical understanding through openness and grace.

The more we live in and through that love, and turn away from judgment, bitterness and negativity, the more our hearts are set free.

Embrace your heart moments by simply being aware of what has broken, disappointed or confused your soul.

Even in the midst of abundant challenges, we are given a chance to heal our heart through what we tell ourselves and how we say it.

Remember the mantra: everyone has a story. Well, that includes YOU.

Don't let a heart moment go by without truly opening your mind to what so beautifully guides your soul.

And remember, it's OK to let your heart live on the outside of you.

It's in those precious moments that we truly understand what unconditional love is – words and actions included.

SEA LEGS

When we are starting anything new - a job, relationship, schedule, commute - it is only natural to feel like we don't quite have our sea legs yet.

Newness can make our steps feel unsteady.   Feeling a lack of confidence makes us question so much about the innermost recesses of our hearts.

But you know what?   Each new experience will only be new once.

If you can somehow keep your feet firmly planted on the ground in and through the newness, you will discover how to keep moving forward.

And once the newness wears off? You will find a wonderful gift -the development of a deeper part of our soul.

Will you stumble and fall? Yes. But you will also learn how to get back up stronger than you ever were before.

Decide today to loyally love the newness and to not be intimidated.

It's in the stumbling and falling that makes getting back up so very worth it.

SOUL SOURCE

Do not find your confidence in the people you date, the jobs you hold, the grades on your report card, the equity in your home or the number on the scale.

Those are all fleeting. They don't define the passion within you.

Do not try to be someone you are not.

Do not listen to the negative spin around you.

Do not compare anything about you or your life to someone else.

Embrace the experiences of your journey as the tough, challenging life-changing lessons that they are.

Realize you will keep repeating some lessons until you learn them once and for all.

And yes, that means you might have to retake a test or two.

Ready to repeat the mantra?

You are beautiful.   Repeat: I am beautiful.

You are unique.   Repeat: I am unique.

You are authentic.   Repeat: I am authentic.

You deserve loyal love.   Repeat: I deserve loyal love.

WHAT WE HEAR

Why do we listen to someone else's opinion about our daily lives?

Why are we swayed to change the way we think or how we act based on a trend or what is popular?

Self-confidence has absolutely nothing to do with popularity or opinion and everything to do with authenticity and grace.

When we get silent enough to hear our own heartbeat, we will also have the space to listen to our OWN thoughts.

When we stop worrying about how someone will react to us and instead let our reactions be straight from our soul, the walls we have built around our egos will slowly start to crumble.

It won't happen at one time, but once we allow ourselves to be silent, we also give ourselves the ability to listen.

And once we listen, we may be surprised to learn how much we really do have to say.

TURNING POINT

Turning point. Look at your past as just that: the past.

Your past does not define you. The circumstances you once faced only applied to that stage of your life.

What once held you back can now set you free. Let that sink in for a minute.

Staring fear in the face and finding the courage to leap into uncharted territory is what the journey to self-respect is all about.

One step at a time, heart pounding, find the strength within you, to turn the corner and be free.

As you listen to the rhythm of your spirit, as you gain strength from every new decision, take a big, deep breath.

Release all the negative energy, doubts, and mistruths. Know that the journey towards loyal love is all about the turning points. Right or left – just keep moving.

Whatever you are facing right now is teaching you how to loyally love yourself. So go ahead- try it. Own your tears, smiles and everything in between.

Trust the fact that when you come to the end of all light of all you know, you WILL be given wings to fly.

REST UP

Some days it's OK to simply feel weary.

Medical challenges, unexpected bills, technology glitches, broken down cars, endless work deadlines, the physical limits of our bodies, spiritual depletion, end of year school projects - the list goes on.

But even through the weariness, there is hope.

When you do what you love, without complaint, but with a spirit of loyal love, you will find the energy you have been missing. Even when your schedule is packed with more events than anyone could possibly imagine, take the time to rest.

Ask for help if you need it. Say "no" to a request now and then, take time for yourself, and keep finding reasons to smile every day.

Stop worrying about what others think - such thoughts will only increase that weariness. Instead, close your eyes, look into your heart (not the calendar on your phone), and simply be present.

No matter where this day finds you or what situation you are facing, seek rest throughout your day.

It's when we can recognize our choices build our outlook that we can truly find peace in all we say and do.

CHILDLIKE WONDER

When we are children, we are simply told to be ourselves.

Childlike joy, faith, and energy are precious qualities that guide our early days and teach us about who we are and what is important to us.

Over time, however, we stop remembering this simple phrase. We lose ourselves in life's circumstances, or what other people think, or on the screen in front of our faces. We stop focusing on all that is good and instead turn inward to the challenges in our day.

Stop turning inward.

Loyal love is about looking up and finding your childlike wonder again.

Believe in who you are for this very moment in time, without judgment, without condition, and without fear. Take in and on the world around you. Offer someone a smile. Send a note to someone you care about.

Give hugs just as you did when you were a preschooler. The world is full of wonder. Childlike wonder that is there for the offering.

Don't be afraid to express exactly who you are and what is in your heart. When we get out of ourselves, our thoughts, grievances, joy, faith, and energy will return our feet to a healthy path of self-confidence once again.

ENGAGED SPIRIT

Self-confidence begins with an engaged spirit and a connected heart.

Honor your passions by always putting in the effort without worrying about the result. Even when everything isn't going the way you had originally hoped or anticipated, you can still find joy in the journey itself.

There will be carefree days, and there will be frustrating days.

There will be days when everything makes perfect sense, and there will be days that leave you scratching your head and wondering what it all means.

But through every point of your journey, as your spirit continues to engage and your heart connects to what is good, celebrate what life is teaching you.

Lean into your faith, concentrate on what you can change for the better and let go of the rest.

So as your head hits the pillow this evening, remember how much you are loyally loved. Rest your eyes, engage your spirit and connect to your heart.

Believe you can and you will.

TRUST THE LESSON

It's amazing how the words of advice you give to others are often needed for your own spirit.

When life's circumstances are more difficult than you ever imagined, that is when there are great and poignant lessons to be learned.

When someone stops believing in you, or the nature of your heart, or decides to turn away from all that you knew, that's where your faith, love, and compassion come in, not only for the situation at hand but for yourself.

When you feel tested, when your emotions are right on the surface, take a breath, say a prayer, and let it all go.

One foot in front of the other, you will find strength.

One foot in front of the other, you will find hope.

One foot in front of the other, you will find your way to exactly the path you were meant to be on.

Find your voice. Follow your heart. And believe that everything happens for a reason. Tough advice, to be sure, but the peace that surpasses all aspects of loyal love and self-respect is real.

You just have to open your eyes wide enough to find it.

IT'S NOT ABOUT YOU

Has someone ever cut you off or completely out of their lives?

Did someone you once trusted with your deepest thoughts stopped talking to you for reasons you cannot possibly figure out?

Have you been waiting for a friend to return a text or phone call?

Have you ever been ghosted and left to wonder why?

Chances are, at one time or another in your life, this has happened to you. And you need to hear this. On repeat.

It's not about you.

Cowardice is a form of emotional cruelty. Ignoring someone's feelings and pretending like they no longer exist says so much more about another person's character than your own.

Will it hurt your heart? Absolutely.

Will you feel empty, alone or confused? Yes.

But know this: People who leave your life without any warning or any explanation are NOT worth your tears.

Keep reading to learn how to find your smile again. And you will find your smile. One loyal love lesson at a time.

YOU ARE NEVER ALONE

Through every celebration and every heartache, you are never alone.

As you journey down the path of unconditional self-respect, you are finding out exactly where you belong.

In knowing your own heart, you will find strength beyond all measure, protection surrounded in almighty grace and eternal hope for the future.

Even when things don't quite add up, when the path you thought you were following changes and when there is a senseless tragedy, you are never alone.

When things get out of balance, when priorities are a bit out of sorts, when you are overcome by fear or frustration, remember to keep trusting that small steady voice.

Through the tears and the smiles, trust the loyal love found in your own heart. It will lead you right where you are supposed to be.

Over time, you will find your center again, your true north, and with it more love, peace and joy than you ever thought possible.

TAKE THE HIGH ROAD

In the depths of your deepest disappointments, there is always hope.

In the darkest corners of your pain, there is mercy.

In the tears that flow down your face, there is an honest understanding of your heart.

We all have a story behind the sparkle in our eyes, the wrinkles on our face and the scars of our soul.

Every day we can strive to be the best version of ourselves we know how to be - rooted in unconditional respect, grace and kindness that knows no boundaries.

Attempt to take the high road, be gentle with yourself and your tender spirit, and always remember, even on the days when your world feels like it has been turned upside down; you can choose words and actions of loyal love.

Be tender with your own spirit. Keep your heart open and your mind aware. When gentle throws you a few curveballs, make the most of every at-bat.

Loyally loving who you are is a journey, learning from your failures and adjusting as you go.

CHOOSE HAPPY

Ask for support as you need it or even before you reach that point.

Never stop believing there is goodness in each person, even when it's difficult to see at times.

Do not grow weary or heavyhearted. Embrace the lessons of the journey. For when you least expect it, goodness will come.

Goodness will come.

Even when others may try to intimidate you or build themselves up by putting you down, you can decide to loyally love yourself. On the days when the behaviors and words of those you used to hold dear don't match, you can still choose happy.

Decide, right here and now, to turn away from bitterness and pain. Focus on what you have learned, the strength you have gained, and the ability to listen to that small steady voice, knowing all the while, that it will not misguide you.

Your instincts are powerful, poignant, and if we are honest with ourselves, they are usually telling us exactly what we need to hear, believe and accept.

So as the sun sets on another day and the anticipation of morning draws near, be aware of each emotion you are having.

It's when we can LISTEN to what is in the depths of our heart and the whisperings of our soul, that it is far easier to get back on the path we are destined for, one thoughtful step at a time.

TURN AWAY FROM DARKNESS

If you are open to the warmth and beauty of the light, turning away from darkness is simply about seeking the truth.

As you approach the Fire, beauty will rise from the ashes one decision at a time. Recognize when you are at your most vulnerable, some days will feel like your lowest point, your rock bottom.

Learning the art of loyal love is based on this simple rule: we can always choose to begin again.

Mercies are NEW every morning, and it is in facing the Fire, in going THROUGH and not around, you are being shaped the most.

The challenge is to let your steps be guided one day at a time, throughout each point of your journey. Stop running away or putting on a mask that isn't who you truly are when things get tough.

Don't fear the Fire. Walk to it and take in the warmth of its forgiveness and mercy and lessons.

Apologize as you need and focus on a new beginning. Don't just speak the words, but take a step, every day, towards the vision you want, need and desire.

Be open to the truth and let it become a part of you. You will be amazed at how much light you will find when you turn away from your darkness and into the loving arms of Hope, Grace, and Love.

TIMEOUT

When's the last time you put yourself in timeout?

Most of the time, we keep pushing, moving forward, striving for man-made measures of success.

But amid our lofty goals and varied achievements, we grow weary. Tired. Worn down. Discouraged.

Today's lesson of loyal love is about hitting the pause button. Why not let your success be measured by how your soul feels when you slow down, cut back and rest?

True victory will present itself when you relax, regroup and allow yourself to take a long, deep breath.

In a society that's constantly pushing us to do more, take the time to enjoy the quiet moments and listen to the innermost recesses of your heart.

You may be pleasantly surprised about the peace you feel when you allow yourself to be present in the moment at hand simply and freely.

Recognize the rest you need and feel the achievement of that recognition.

Even if it's only for a few minutes, put yourself in a loyal love timeout today.

JOY WILL FOLLOW

Joy follows gratitude.

What a simple, yet powerful reminder.

Breathe in the goodness of the day, take in that which energizes your soul, brings you comfort, and think about what you learned from every experience, person, or circumstance that you encountered today.

Like a preschooler with never-ending curiosity, it's OK to wonder why things happen when and how they do.

But even in the wondering, you can focus on what you were grateful for this very day, no matter how it played out.

In focusing on true joy - hope, peace, and grace can be yours for many seasons to come.

Release all you can't control or understand. Truly let go in order to loyally love yourself.

After a difficult day, when facing impossible circumstances or people, if you are simply worn down by all which you are facing, don't forget to focus on all the blessings in your life.

Positive energy is contagious. So tomorrow, before your feet hit the floor, remember to focus on at least one thing you are thankful for. It could change the course of your entire day.

Remember the power of loyal love.

LIFT ONE ANOTHER UP

How is love replaced in someone's heart with hate? What removes mercy and empathy from a person's soul?

The more we exclude one another, the more we judge or dismiss or ignore who someone is - the more risk we have of separating ourselves from all that is good, kind, necessary, and true.

When someone cuts you out of their life without explanation, it can feel like a balloon suddenly being popped and the pieces of the balloon quickly falling to the ground.

Lift one another up in word and deed. Always.

Display kindness in thought, word, and action. And even when your opinions or stances differ from the thoughts or actions of someone else, be respectful.

If there are senseless acts of inexplicable violence, find peace in giving, receiving, and living a life of unconditional loyal love.

Keep talking with hearts filled with forgiveness and grace. Stand together in peace.

As your head hits the pillow and you drift into sleep, pray that the world will be a kinder, gentler, and more compassionate place when you open your eyes in the morning.

DO NOT FEAR THE UNKNOWN

Do not fear the unknown.

Do not shy away from the light.

Instead, walk towards the warmth of the sunshine, putting your darkest nights and greatest challenges behind you.

Lean into the strength of self-respect if you don't have the energy to stand tall. Insults may be hurled. Truths misconstrued. Your heart may hurt. Your body may feel worn. Your spirit may be burdened.

But you are enough – just the way you are.

Through perfect grace, the past is the past. It cannot be undone. Learn from your history and simply do the very best you can.

Today is a new day.

You are stronger than any words or actions against you. In learning to loyally love yourself, you are conquering your fear of the unknown. Just take a step out of faith. Inch by inch, TRUST.

Even if you can't see the path before you, move closer to the light of loyal love for yourself and even those who persecute you.

As you place your feet gently to the floor today and as you rest your head on your pillow tonight, know that the more you let go, the more you will journey towards self-respect: one day, hour and moment at a time.

WHAT YOU REALLY NEED

Compromises.

Sometimes it's not about focusing on what we are giving up, but what we are gaining in the process.

In the emptying of ourselves, in saying yes to others and no to self, we get to know the deepest part of our souls.

In finding the balance of what is reasonable vs. narrowing our view to personal reason, we find the truth.

In understanding what works for the very situation that we are going through not only as it applies to us, but as it affects others, we truly find our voice again. With each deep conversation we have, we gain strength.

When connection trumps pride, we grow. When we shut down our devices, our egos, and our own agendas, we truly show how much we value those we love the most.

As we listen, we share so much more about our character than we realize. As we open our hearts and minds, we truly get closer and closer to becoming exactly the person we are supposed to be.

So as the evening winds down and as we process the day and all of its intricacies, remember this: sometimes not getting everything you want is exactly what you need.

BUMPS IN THE ROAD

Continue to marvel at the true power of forgiveness, work through and not around, and remember that everyone has a story.

Page by page, the stories of our lives will unfold exactly as they are supposed to be written.

The less we judge, the more we can listen to those stories.

The less resentment we harbor, the more peace we can find.

The less bitterness we carry in our hearts, the more we can be open to unconditional self-respect, filled with grace and mercy.

Sometimes releasing the hurt is the only way you can honestly turn the page. Truly, you cannot control other people's behaviors or words, only your reactions to them.

As we get older and learn more about life, indeed the most beautiful relationships we will have are ones that have hit a few bumps in the road but still managed to follow those twists and turns to a new path.

Know that it's never too late to work through and not around. Let today be the day that you decide to look up and beyond yourself.

Realize that in saying no to self, you are teaching all those around you about the greatest gift possible: unconditional self-respect.

GRAVITATE TOWARDS LIGHT

Attitudes.

In times of stress, disappointments, challenges, misunderstandings and change, we can easily allow our entire outlook to lean towards the negative side.

Or, we can choose to be happy.

When we let go of all that weighs us down, when we release our worries, when we simply trust that we will be pointed down the right path, when we believe that good things will happen and happen soon, we will once again find our joy.

The power to change our attitude in the difficult moments is how we grow. We can choose to gravitate towards the light and goodness of each day and take the weight of the world from our shoulders, especially since we are often the one who put it there, to begin with.

As a new season draws near, when our daily schedules may soon be adjusting to having kids home, or planning a vacation, or balancing sports schedules, or figuring out a way to build in downtime, let us remember the mercies we show ourselves can be NEW every morning.

No matter what we are facing, we can choose to be happy in the process.

FINISH YOUR RACE

Even when you're going through something that frustrates or confuses you, taking the high road is always the best path.

Throughout the most challenging of circumstances, showing compassion towards others will bring you a peace that surpasses all understanding.

With a spirit of humility, kindness and grace, learn from the lessons of your journey, let go of all you don't understand and finish your race stronger than you ever thought possible.

In everything you do, no matter the circumstances, history, hurt, confusion or frustration, treat others the way you want to be treated.

Choose your words carefully, let your actions be full of integrity and honor, and respect yourself enough to know when it is simply time to walk away.

Whether you have known someone for 25 years or 25 days, be kind, respectful and loving.

If someone is avoiding a situation or blaming you instead of taking responsibility for their own words and actions, there is much more to their cowardice than meets the eye.

As your feet hit the floor and you embrace the gift of a brand-new day, may you be true to your heart and feel surrounded by a circle of unconditional self-respect, treating others the way you want to be treated, no matter what.

IMPERFECTLY PERFECT

Everyone makes errors in judgment, circumstance and relationships.

If someone stands upon a perch of self-righteousness, chances are they have not yet made progress towards their journey of loyal love or entertained any thoughts of unconditional self-respect.

Don't worry about someone else's imperfections.

Own your mistakes. Learn from them.

And most importantly, don't beat yourself up - what's done is done.

If there are people in your circle who can't deal with your imperfections, go be imperfect around someone who does.

You can get bitter or you can better. Choose the latter. The most beautiful parts of our journey are the moments that make us the most human.

Love unconditionally. Smile more. And embrace every imperfect step along the way.

DON'T LET THE GHOSTS DEFINE YOU

You are not defined by those who choose to disappear from your life.

Repeat.

You are NOT defined by those who choose to disappear from your life.

But, oh, how the heart aches when your head can't make sense of a sudden and permanent loss.

It can happen with friendships, family members, boyfriends, girlfriends or even those you thought you could trust the most.

Remember that their decisions, however painful or inexplicable, say volumes about their own character and NOTHING about yours.

Stop trying to get the answers you will never receive.

Instead, keep your head up, your shoulders back and know the people who WANT to actively be in your life will do just that.

Find strength in knowing ghosting is a selfish act and you are stronger from the lesson of a sudden departure.

Keep being true to you, moving forward and reminding yourself that when one person leaves your life, you are simply making room for a new one.

After all, Casper was only a cartoon. Leave the ghosts in your past and walk towards the path of unconditional self-respect.

VULNERABLE AUTHENCITY

There is something to be said about unconditionally loving yourself with a spirit of self-respect.

It begins with being honest. Real. Vulnerable. Authentic.

Honoring your authentic self and being aware enough to know when you have hurt someone, apologize for your actions or words, and to not avoid the uncomfortable parts, is key to how we grow.

Going through and not around is how we learn, and ultimately, how we reach the next level of self-awareness. Talking things through, saying you are sorry, even writing out your innermost thoughts, is often a difficult process, but with a heart full of grace, a willing and open spirit, and casting all judgment aside, it can be done.

When there's a fork in the road, a decision point, you can be open to the path ahead of you or be suffocated and sentenced by a life you never really embraced as your own.

How you approach the gift of each morning can either lighten your load with hope or weigh you down. Condemned by past choices, stifle the direction of your own personal journey, or be set free.

BEGIN AGAIN

Every day is a beautiful opportunity for a new beginning.

When we focus more on showing one another love, kindness, grace, respect, understanding, and mercy and less on judgment, criticism, sensitivity, and selfishness, life is truly filled with endless possibilities and adventures.

Stop walking on eggshells and be EXACTLY the person you were meant to be.

Say what is in your heart, treat others as you wish to be treated, and know when it's simply time to let go, move forward, and never look back.

The good news about going through, however painful and confusing, is that being true to who you are, and being comfortable enough to express that in its entirety, can bring you closer to the peace, joy, and love that genuine self-respect surrounds you with every day.

Your mercies can be new every morning when you choose the path to loyal love.

The more we say no to selfishness, and yes to self-respect, the happier and more at peace we will be.

RESOLVE TO BE HAPPY

Resolve to be happy, no matter the circumstances or situation.

As your life moves forward, so do the lessons. Lift one another up in word and in action.

Focus on honoring what's in your heart, mind and soul, take the high road, stay humble and remember that today is a brand-new opportunity to simply turn the page and start again.

Never put the power of your happiness in a situation or relationship. Both will eventually disappoint you. The best way to show loyalty to your own heart is by honoring your journey of self-respect.

Dedicate yourself, every day, to finding simple reasons to smile.

It could be sipping on your favorite coffee or appreciating the air in your lungs.

Remember the beauty of self-reflection is this: when you can identify all your discouragements, heartbreaks, confusions and toxic people and circumstances, you can find happiness in letting them go.

Resolve to be happy.

TRUST YOUR GUT

Never limit your dreams with fear of the unknown.

If you can imagine the potential for what will be, you have already started your journey towards reaching your new summit.

When you come to the end of all that is familiar, your steadfast self-respect will meet you on your path and gently direct your steps, however kindly they need to be taken.

So on this day as you journey towards loyal love, challenge yourself right out of your normal comfort zone.

Believe that you can. Dream that you will. Imagine the life that will bring you a peace that surpasses all understanding. Then make some practical choices.

Listen to your heart. Connect with a mentor. Grab a friend for a cup of coffee.

Instead of focusing on your limitations, know that you can achieve the musings of your soul.

Simply trust the small steady voice that guides your heart. Say "yes"' to knowing that even when the road is unclear, there is a new and beautiful path awaiting you, one small step at a time.

ACKNOWLEDGE WHAT HURTS

Be brave enough to acknowledge what hurts, be humble enough to apologize for it, and begin to allow great healing into your head and within your heart.

Relationships, in all their forms, are precious. Truly, some are seasonal, and some will last a lifetime, but they all require grace, vulnerability, and tender care.

Remember that the root of most misunderstandings is simply individual interpretations or raw reactions in the given moment.

Protect yourself as you need and communicate what is important to you, but do not harden the core of who you are.

Find the blessing in going through and not around. Stop avoiding challenges or sweeping things under the table.

The path to self-respect is going through, shedding tears and reminding yourself you are human.

Continue to keep it real. Push forward towards the path to healing, and take the first step in acknowledging that each person who enters our lives has a purpose for being there.

Find self-confidence in knowing that through our authenticity, we become even closer to the truth that loyal love is all about.

STOP COMPLAINING

In every circumstance and every situation, you can find the humor, positivity, and lesson if you pause, gather your thoughts, let go of all that you don't understand, and quickly turn the page.

Life is always going to be a series of ups and downs. It is how you respond through BOTH the successes and the adversities that build strong character.

Trust the process.

On good days. On bad days. And on days when your frustration level has the potential to reach new heights.

Breathe.

Count your blessings.

Surround yourself with a supportive circle who will listen without judgment and give you an encouraging smile, nod, or word.

Stop complaining about what you don't have and give thanks for what you do. Know tomorrow is a new day filled with promise, mercy, and grace.

Embrace your future of loyal love.

Without regret, open your heart, mind, and soul to the goodness, love, and beauty of what lies ahead - one self-respect focused step at a time.

EMBRACE THE DAY

That insecure, unsure, shy person from high school, college or your first terrible job?

That person is part of your past.

They were defined by the opinion of others. You grew stronger despite the opinions.

They were led by a naivety and inexperience. You matured because of the experiences and look at the world with realistic glasses.

They were afraid of what tomorrow would bring. You are more than ready to put your hands on your hips in a Superman or Superwoman pose and embrace the endless possibilities of your future.

When you live life through the lens of loyal love and when you move towards the path to learning the art of unconditional self-respect, you will be free.

Every day is a beautiful opportunity for a new beginning of loyal love.

Embrace the day.

KEEP DREAMING

There is something to be said about the loyalty you show to your own heart and mind when you dream big and keep working towards making those dreams a reality.

If someone tells you "no," show them how you live from the spirit of "yes."

There's something to be said about diligently working hard towards turning your dreams into a reality.

Dedication. Character. Perseverance.

All these qualities teach us, change us, encourage us and inspire us. When we know better, we do better.

Sometimes the toughest chapters in our lives are designed to promote us to the next level through integrity, grace and self-respect.

Learn from your challenges, stay humble through your success and continue to inch forward, no matter what obstacles may slow you down for a while.

Put in the work, believe the best, stay positive, give it all you got and never give up on your dreams.

At the end of the day, that is what loyal love is about.

MOVE FORWARD

Never be afraid to make that first move towards an even deeper level of loyal love.

Your heart understands what is true. Know that the path you are destined for isn't the same one that is right for your neighbors, friends, or relatives. Nor should it be.

Like a toddler learning to walk, each child learns how to take steps at the pace that works for them. Remember that it's ok to stagger a bit, falter as and when you should, and sometimes fall a few times.

It's in the second attempt or the third or the fourth that you will learn great lessons. It is in brushing yourself off and finding your balance, that one step turns into two.

As Kris Kringle tells the Winter Warlock, sometimes you just must "put one foot in front of the other and soon you'll be walking out the door."

Take the first step.

Even when it scares you the most. Dare greatly and without limitations. Find the path that was designed to give you great value, bring peace to your soul, and happiness to your being.

No matter how small, if you focus on the blessings of that first move, you will one day look back and wonder what took you so long to journey towards self-respect

ALREADY APPROVED

Everyone has a story.

Some people embrace their stories and with every life experience, find their voice in the process. They say what they mean, and their actions mirror their words.

They aren't afraid to be vulnerable. Because in and through that vulnerability, they find the greatest gift they will ever know - inner truth.

Some people, however, create a less authentic tale - one guided by the constant need for approval.

They present a side of themselves that is one-dimensional, often only saying what they think others want to hear, or worse yet, judging someone who has followed a different path than their own.

Challenge yourself, dear friends, to get to know your inner truth.

No matter what you are facing, whatever circumstance or whatever hurts, it truly is in the going through that we learn, grown, and evolve.

Love with your whole heart, take risks, make mistakes, and write the pages of each beautiful chapter.

One moment at a time, you are already approved.

AUTHENTIC TRUTH

The importance of character, loyalty and self-respect is understood through our vulnerable ability to be authentic.

If our words do not match our actions or our actions do not match our words, we are only doing ourselves a disservice.

Self-respect has a foundation of authenticity.

It does not hide when times are rough.

It does not create a false truth when the facts speak for themselves.

It does not get angry when the people you once called friends now perch themselves on a branch of self-righteousness.

The gift of loving ourselves through disappointments and heartbreak - through the things that don't make sense while we are facing them at the moment - this is how we grow.

Finding inner peace, knowing when it's time to walk away from unhealthy people or situations and understanding the beauty and fragility of our own self-esteem - that is learning the art of unconditional self-respect.

WHEN ENOUGH IS ENOUGH

There comes a point in many relationships when you must decide.

Do you like the way you are being treated?

Are you at peace with your own actions and words when you are around that person?

Or do you find yourself being someone you are not?

Do you tell yourself they probably didn't mean to hurt your feelings?

Are you wiping away more tears than during allergy season?

Then chances are – for yourself – for your heart – and for all you deserve – it may be time to walk away.

People will make a thousand excuses all day long - but the fact of the matter is - everyone has the same 24 hours in a day and the same seven days in a week.

Everyone has choices -- decisions in how they spend their time, who they spend it with and how they treat others along the way.

Don't be a doormat. Stand up for yourself, let go of who and what doesn't give you energy and know when enough is enough.

FIND YOUR COURAGE

Breathe in all that lightens your worries, brings peace to your spirit and reminds you of what is truly important.

Let go of the rest.

Surround yourself with unconditional self-respect through a circle of support that encompasses the good, the bad and the ugly.

Be around those who will make the time for the ordinary days as much as the special occasions, not create excuses about they why's, when's and why nots.

Protect what you value and seek tranquility in knowing you often learn the most by taking a few awkward steps backward before you can confidentially move forward again.

As you journey towards loyal love, accept the things that you cannot change, find the courage to change the things you can, and rely on the wisdom of that small steady voice deep within your heart that somehow always knows the difference.

LOVE THROUGH THE PAIN

The importance of character, authenticity, and the gift of loving yourself through disappointments, heartbreak and the things that don't make sense while we are facing them at the moment - that is the very definition of healthy self-respect.

Finding inner peace, knowing when it's time to walk away from unhealthy people or situations and understanding the beauty and fragility of our own self-worth can be a lifelong process.

Loyal unconditional love is about learning to love yourself through, during and around.

Don't let someone else take away your joy.

Instead, find your smile - one moment at a time.

There are those who know what you do for your job, sport or hobby and there are those who understand how and why your passions drive you.

There are those who know where you came from and there are those who understand how your former fears and insecurities still tend to shape your words and actions.

There are those who know your surface level and there are those who take the time to fully understand the complex layers of your mind, heart and soul.

Be thankful for those who know you, but love you through the pain: today, tomorrow and always.

CONTROL YOURSELF

"You cannot control the behaviors, thoughts, and actions of another, but you can control your reactions to them." ~ Joyce Meyer

Allow yourself to know most people are simply trying to do the best they can, as they are, and as life comes. Authentically flawed and beautifully human - during the good days and the bad, we are all imperfect and learning as we go.

Realize our paths are ever changing. Make mistakes and learn from those mistakes. When we know better, we do better.

Don't judge; listen. Don't cast the first stone, but instead offer to help.

Every person you know is going through something - living out their own stories, at a pace that is right for them.

As we move forward - without a magic wand to heal those battling horrible health issues, or to give peace to those whom are struggling with relationships or to instill confidence in those who have lost their hope- let go and loyally love who you are.

Go through and not around. Know it's ok to be tired, to rest, and to regroup when you finally want to acknowledge the fragility of your soul.

HIT THE BRAKES

Know your limits. Did you hear that? SLOW DOWN.

When your body tells you to walk instead of run, listen.

When your soul whispers that you need alone time or a few days at the ocean, take it.

When your mind longs for meditation or prayer, be silent.

In an age of technology and always feeling like we need to respond, it may be difficult to unplug and turn off the devices, but it's also downright necessary.

Sometimes what we actually need at our very core is to take our foot off the gas pedal, take a few deep breaths, reconnect to what we love and just be.

Try this act of self-respectful kindness. Let your yes mean yes and your no mean no from the moment of your initial response.

And if you feel overwhelmed? Try again.

Get plenty of sleep, drink lots of water, exercise your mind and soul and exhale.

Self-respect is about the daily commitment of being kind to yourself in every possible way.

Starting. Now.

BE THE EXAMPLE

Find your value in knowing the journey to loyal love has a foundation of self-respect. It is this place of value that will build up your heart, mind and spirit through every decision you make over the rest of your life.

Even when you can't see or feel immediate changes, even when the silence is deafening, even when it feels like the hurt will never end – remind yourself of these loyal love truths:

You are worthy.

You are loved.

You are cherished.

When those around you focus on themselves, don't follow their example.

Instead, connect to the world with your whole heart and know that such loyal love will one day be met be a circle of unconditional support.

Keep walking through the doors that only a journey of self-respect can open. Keep looking out the window and letting your life be filled by the goodness, kindness and grace that will be returned to you a thousand-fold.

Know you are seen.

Know you are heard.

Know you are loved.

TRUST THE MASTER PLAN

Do you think they can't see your heart as it breaks in two?
Look into the recesses of your heart to heal.

Do you think they care if you are frustrated or confused?
Look into your motivations to find clarity.

Do you think they wonder what you've been through?
Look into your experiences and know you are stronger because of them.

Do you think words said to put you down make you less of a person?
Look into your own story to find the path to loyal love.

Letting go is part of the master plan. You know that. They may not. Even
when all you want to do is hide, be bold. You are learning the art of
unconditional self-respect.

Open your mind, heart and soul as you grow from the very tears they caused.

And believe that someday – they will walk the path to loyal love just like you
did.

LIVE DEEPER

Sometimes the greatest rewards can be found through the big, beautiful, never-ending circle of communication: both sharing and listening.

When you take the time to open up and get real, when you share the deepest recesses of your heart, it's amazing how much you can learn.

Stop closing yourself off and living life on the surface.

Go deeper. Be vulnerable.

When you ask someone else how they are doing, wait for more than a one-word answer.

As the saying goes, people are often fighting battles you know nothing about. Why? Because we sometimes get too inward focused to notice.

Remind yourself that investing a listening ear and an open non-judgmental heart is the best way to truly learn about compassion, forgiveness and grace – not just for others, but for yourself too.

Today's lesson of loyal love is about your greatest reward. All you need to do is take a deep breath, listen from your heart and when the time is right, respond with kindness, mercy and unconditional self-respect.

PUSH THE LIMITS

Recognizing your limits is not a sign of weakness.

Even through the most paralyzing of circumstances, striving towards a harmonious balance of the heart, mind, body, and spirit is often the greatest challenge we may ever know.

A fresh start can point you down the path to inner peace and give you the energy and strength to keep moving forward.

Acknowledge what overwhelms you. Make changes, even if they are small ones, to do something about it.

No matter the age or experience, strength comes from being aware of your current reality and resetting expectations and actions accordingly.

As one of my favorite quotes states, "A journey of a thousand miles begins with a single step." ~ Lao Tsu

Let today's loyal love act be about carving out a time of self-reflection, finding hope in knowing good can be found in pausing to recognize your limits.

Once you do, you can make positive changes with humility, understanding, and grace.

DON'T BE A SHEEP

Why is ghosting even a thing?

Because it is easier for some people to sheepishly vanish from your life without a word or the courtesy of a conversation instead of talking through any points of confusion, misunderstanding or hurt.

People are selfish. And we live in a drive-through age.

They don't want to put the time into working through. They want to go around, keep things on the surface and avoid their emotions.

If you have been abandoned at any point in your life - by a parent, teacher, friend, partner or loved one - you know how much ghosting can bring up ALL of those empty feelings.

But take heart.

Ghosting is NOT about you. It's about THEM. If you have done all you can do - asked for answers - wanted to talk things through - leave things on a positive note - and there is STILL no response - know that life can move on.

Let your ghosts disappear into your past.

Be strong. Be brave. Do not take things personally.

Know that the best way to loyally love yourself is by learning the art of unconditional self-respect.

AVOID THE ICEBERG

If you have ever watched the movie Titanic, did you ever wonder how on earth the captain of the ship didn't see what was coming?

Icebergs can sink a ship even when there is a trained professional at the wheel.

Don't judge the captain of the ship, especially when the captain of life's vessel is you.

Accidents are a part of life. Even with hours of endless training, sometimes you are going to make mistakes.

If you don't see the iceberg in time to avoid it, deal with your heart, mind and soul after the impact has happened.

Upright the ship and steer clear of the drama that once defined your lack of knowing who you are and what you deserve.

And remember - it's a beautiful thing when you take the time to understand the cracks and scars that go to the very foundation of loyal love.

The more you understand who you are, the bigger the raft you will have to safely make it to the island of unconditional self-respect.

LISTEN UP

Listening to what your body, mind, and spirit are telling you is so immensely important to every chapter of your life.

Sometimes it starts as a whisper and then before you know it, the whisper gets louder until you are truly knocked off your feet by the steady voice telling you, demanding you, to loyally love who you are.

Sometimes the message is about your limits: Physical. Emotional. Mental.

What will it take for you to start paying attention? A trip to the ER? A lost friendship? A restless night of sleep?

Be grateful to the voices you hear. The words are usually a poignant reminder to take better care of yourself.

Ready to start listening?

Following the path to self-respect has a beautiful and helpful message.

All you have to do is take the time to stop talking and start understanding – loyal love will show you the way.

YOU CAN DO THIS

The small and steady voice deep within your soul will always tell you when it's time to walk away from a negative situation or person.

Whether you have known that individual for three months or thirty years, if you aren't being treated with kindness, love and respect, there is nothing wrong with turning away and moving on.

The further you walk away from their negative influence, the greater space you create for a healthy and happy chapter to begin.

Will it be challenging? You bet.

But do not make excuses.
Do not lean into what's comfortable.
Do not blame others or lash out from a place of fear, anger, or pride.

Accept where you are on your journey and find the courage to know there will be healthy and loving relationships in your life when you loyally love yourself first.

You can do this.

As difficult as it is, you are not alone. Is it not time to love yourself as much as you love others? What are you waiting for? Get up, brush yourself off, and take the first beautiful step of your loyal love journey.

CUT UP THE MEASURING TAPE

Our worth cannot and should not be summarized in numbers.

It cannot be measured by our bank account balance or the number staring up at us from the scale below. The template used on a grading curve or our performance rating at work never truly captures our entire story.

Rather, our value comes from the satisfaction we feel after a long heart-to-heart conversation where both parties are respected and heard, or the twinkle in our children's eyes when they understand a concept or read their first words.

Our worth comes from the great peace in our hearts when we follow the path we are supposed to take, and from celebrating not just the big moments, but the little ones too.

Our significance is established through the energy we create in being kind to others and expecting nothing in return.

So on this day of loyal love, take a few minutes to release the metrics that have any power over you. Let go of the numbers that guide your day. Instead, let your heart be filled with unconditional love, grace and mercy.

As the wise Maya Angelou once said, "Life is not measured by the number of breaths you take, but by the moments that take your breath away."

QUIET THE DOUBTS

When the doubts creep in, how do you keep moving down the path of self-worth?

When you are facing an unexpected challenge or when life throws you a few curveballs, how do you understand that it's ok to strike out a few times?

By dusting yourself off and getting UP.

If you stay down, you let the doubts win.

Instead, focus on what you know, find one or two positive things to focus on and keep moving forward - knowing that eventually, your perseverance will lead you down the path you are meant to take.

Will some days be completely overwhelming?

Absolutely.

But loyally loving yourself isn't only for one day. It's for a lifetime.

The time is NOW. Get up, brush yourself off and move on.

FIND YOUR EMPATHY

When we let our frustrations drown out what is in our hearts, we get caught up in expectations instead of reality.

Find your empathy by trying to understand where someone else is coming from.

Even when the thoughts, beliefs and actions of those around you don't align with your own, you can show grace, kindness and compassion – first to yourself and then to others.

Sometimes we forget that everyone has a story and we cannot judge someone by the chapter we walked in on or an article that is trending on social media or a news clip from the 11:00 broadcast.

So what can we remember? We can spread a message of love by loyally loving who we are and what we stand for without condemning others in the process.

We can seek understanding by listening when others talk and only responding out of unconditional love.

We can empathize not from our heads, but through and within our hearts.

We can eliminate our apathy by doing more to help through our shared humanity and goodness.

We can do better by knowing better, replacing our ignorance with wisdom, our intolerance with acceptance, and our judgment with loyal love.

OWN YOUR STORY

In learning to love ourselves, we first need to take ownership of our own story.

Your past does not need to define your future, but you do need to take the time to process where you came from, what you have learned and how you want the rest of your chapters to unfold.

Everyone. Has. A. Story.

Before you judge, listen.

Before you assume, ask.

Don't be the darkness in someone else's story.   Instead, be a source of radiant light, gentle truth, and unconditional love, forgiveness, and grace in your own.

As each page of your story is told, take the time to digest every word.   And if something doesn't make sense? Be a detective. Go back and read it again.

Simply remember, the people, experiences, and challenges in our lives don't always tell the entire tale.

You may not have had the start to life that you wanted, but by learning to loyally love yourself, you can still write a beautiful ending.

PATCH IT TOGETHER

Sometimes when we feel at our weakest, that's when we are mastering the stitches to create an enormous quilt of strength.

When we feel at our most broken, that is how learning the art of unconditional self-respect will make our loyal love story – whole.

Each patch of our quilt is slowly sewn from life's experiences, the people we meet, our reactions to them and what we learn along the way.

Triumphs and disappointments.
Frustration and joy.
Sadness and happiness.

Knowing what people say about us or how they act is not what gives us warmth.   From the inside out, what truly comforts our souls is the beautiful blanket made from a tapestry of mercy, grace, understanding and forgiveness.

Building a quilt takes patience, trust, and not necessarily knowing what the finished product will look like.   Each stitch is designed for a specific purpose. And each patch of the quilt needs time to develop its own message.

Keep at it.

Stitch by stitch, the journey to self-respect will bring you more comfort, warmth and love than you ever thought possible.

BE AN ARTIST

When you are in the middle of a challenging, uncomfortable or confusing situation, don't be afraid to go THROUGH the middle of the fire.

Even when you feel like your feet are being singed by the flames, that is when the journey of self-respect shapes the molten internal energy of whatever situation you are facing.

Learn to let go of the blueprint you thought you wanted. Instead, be open to the design you need.

In other words, as you begin to work with the clay, trust your hands enough to mold something new.

And if the original design doesn't turn out the way you thought it would? Throw in some new textures or hues.

Before your head hits the pillow each night, know the flames of the fire will warm your spirit by teaching you the art of loyal love.

When you make it through the fire, you may surprise yourself through the creative expression of who you are and what you are building.

Get your hands dirty by letting your inner artist fly – it's in the middle of the fire, after all, that we can truly understand how beautiful self-respect can be.

CHANGE COURSE

Why is it so challenging to be yourself? Because we all tend to let ourselves get wrapped up in competition of life.

Instead of reaching for the finish line, stop and enjoy the simple pleasure of putting one foot in front of the other.

Nothing more. Nothing less. Just one step at a time.

Your journey will unfold with peace, love and grace when you take the time to acknowledge your passions, honor your interests, face your fears, ignite your dreams, and stop comparing yourself to everybody else.

What makes you laugh, what makes you cry, and what you hold dear is an ever changing story: YOUR story.

Each one of us have different experiences, shaping who we are, how we decide, and what our futures will hold.

Embrace the pages of your story, and when you need to, reread a chapter or two. There's nothing wrong with repeating a lesson until you can accept it as your own.

So as the next moment unfolds, forget about how you thought life was going to go or what you used to expect. The world is flawed, but it is in accepting who we are with a heart of loyal love that a beautiful mess becomes a masterpiece.

Self-respect is about accepting yourself as and where you are. Just be you.

EXPECT THE BEST

Connection is about saying no to society's expectations and yes to the loyal love in your heart.

When you feel down, or when the dreary weather starts to make your soul feel the same way, be determined to focus on what you love.

Connect to that which gives you energy. Grab coffee with a friend. Pick up the phone. Write in a journal or a blog. Take a drive to your favorite thinking place. Watch an old movie or listen to a song that fills your heart with joy.

Reflect on what brings you peace. Understand what you need and don't be afraid to do it. Take the time to listen to that small steady voice leading you down the path you are supposed to journey down.

Look up and outside of yourself. Do something unexpected and kind. Take the time to listen to what is in the innermost recesses of your heart.

Enjoy each and every precious moment, regardless of your circumstances, despite what others say, and how they act towards you.

Connect, reflect, and look up. You'll be amazed how quickly doing so will point you down the path to self-respect - renewing your heart, mind, and soul as you go.

SAY WHAT YOU MEAN

"Be who you are and say what you mean. Because those who mind don't matter and those who matter don't mind!" ~ Dr. Seuss

Dr. Seuss was a very wise man. No truer words have ever been spoken.

Be exactly who you are. Easier said than done. But the older we get, the more we can build a solid foundation of self-respect. In showing loyal love towards ourselves, our words and actions will find their way to a place of peace, grace and gratitude.

Will relationships end throughout your journey? Yes.

People change.
You are changing.

And that is a good thing. Why? Because those who matter the most will accept you as the beautiful mess you are.

If they don't take the time to really get to know you, your heart, and your spirit, then they aren't worth your emotions anyway.

There is a hidden angel inside everyone. It may be clouded by someone's past hurts or selfishness or pride.

But when you focus on learning to love yourself and embrace where you are on the journey, you will truly find the root of happiness.

Even through the tears, loyal love has been there the entire time.

LET THE SHOE DROP

Instead of waiting for the other shoe to drop out of dread or fear, expect something good to happen next.

Go on.

Dare to believe things will get better. It all starts with how you approach your journey of self-respect.

Even on your darkest days, don't go around the hurt, frustration or sadness. Embrace where you are, as you are and who you are with a spirit of loyal love.

Know that even when the shoe does indeed drop, you will have the strength, resilience and trust that you need. Even when you don't understand the situation you are going through, you will be ok.

If you don't want to turn the page quite yet, lean into the next few paragraphs of your life.

Stop concerning yourself with what others think and instead find peace in realizing that through the ups and downs of life, through the successes and disappointments, the only person who can live your life is YOU.

Self-respect is a journey of faith. You may feel like you are lost in the dark, but you can see the light at the end of the tunnel when you decide to look for it.

BLESS YOUR HEART

Abundant blessings are often found in the center of our weakest moments.

While you are often told to focus on what you are grateful for, there is also the reality that waves of grief tend to hit out of nowhere - through a song, a memory, or an empty chair at the dinner table.

Even when you concentrate on counting your blessings, challenge yourself to keep it real instead of trying to create an illusion of perfection.

Let kindness always be the foundation of your words and actions, extending an extra measure of grace, love, and support to those who are hurting.

And if you aren't aware of such hurts? Assume that everybody is going through something - what they share and what they hold within their hearts.

Celebrate our differences by respecting the fact that what may feel like a burden to you can be an abundant blessing to someone else.

When we do the best we can, keep it honest and embrace the imperfect mess we are, we can experience the joy of acceptance, grace, and love that will fill our hearts, minds, and souls.

GET IT STRAIGHT

I'm not talented enough.

I'm not thin enough.

I'm not fashionable enough.

Enough with the enoughs.

Don't let the enough voices get louder. Instead, do something to get rid of them - something you love, something that makes you smile - something that makes you - YOU!

You can find the most peace in truly being open to a new adventure - the adventure of believing in yourself.

Spending time and energy on loving who you are is important for the short and long-term. Not just on the good days, but during the moments when you feel hurt, angry, disappointed or confused - that is the journey to self-respect.

Loyal love is more than enough.

Even when things don't turn out the way you though they would, you will get through it. Even if you need a full day in PJs and a box of tissues, you will find your smile again.

Time to repeat a slightly different mantra:

I am strong.
I am brilliant.
I am more than enough – just the way I am.

FIND YOUR CONFIDENCE

Find your confidence from learning to loyally love the person you are.

What others think or say about you is usually a projection of their own experience or true ignorance about yours.

When someone tells you what you aren't, show them what you are.

When someone tells you that you can't, show them that you can.

Look within the depths of your heart, find out what drives your spirit, and be content in knowing that you are exactly where you should be, as you should be, and how you should be.

And the biggest surprise? You will teach yourself great lessons of inner confidence through a better understanding of what makes you – you.

When you stop worrying about the opinions of other people, your life will truly start to feel free.

Be confident in who you are and what you are learning in this very moment.

Take heart in knowing that even through the most difficult or challenging lessons in life, learning the art of self-respect is a marathon, not a sprint.

To find your confidence, sometimes it is as easy as showing up at the starting line.

REGROUP

Regrouping.

When you simply feel like each day is over before it has begun, or when your behaviors are not lining up with what is in your heart, or when the walls of protection isolate you from the circle you care about the most, take the time to listen to that small steady voice.

Get quiet.
Be still.
And begin again.

The beauty of loyal love is not condemning yourself when things get off. And they will. That's just life.

Each day of self-respect is an open slate just waiting for a lesson to be written, taught and received.

Sometimes we need to let the narrative in our heads turn into background noise.

Regrouping allows you to turn away from attitudes of frustration, confusion or drama, and move closer to the place that brings you peace.

For some, it may mean taking a long walk all by yourself. For others, it could be setting aside time to write in a journal. And for many, simply staring at the ocean and letting the rhythm of the waves match the cadence of your heartbeat may be the way you recharge.

Loyal love is knowing each day is a beautiful opportunity to start again.

REVISE HISTORY

Sometimes it is OK to rewrite history - whether it is your first love or your last. If someone has mistreated you, it's ok to forget the past in order to move on to healthier relationships.

The more we recognize what we need, the more we can show ourselves loyal love by honoring what is in our hearts, minds and souls.

Sometimes we need to stop hoping and start doing.

This may mean resolving what was simply to move closer to your to be. And it also means using your own experiences, yes even the painful ones, to help others.

Own your mistakes, learn from them and move on. The beauty of forgiveness is it encompasses everything, even a broken heart or a silent phone.

Don't ignore someone when they reach out to you.

Listen. Release. Renew.

Continue to share the innermost recesses of your heart.

Every day, move closer to the goal of being whole again, without the need to move backwards towards relationships that were broken. Revise history and be free.

TIME TO PLANT

The empty side of humanity is often without loyal love.

People who lash out are often the ones who haven't taken the time to understand who they are, what they are about and why they say and act a certain way.

When we judge based on hearsay, mistrust based on falsities, and divide ourselves based on personal gain, there is no beauty.

Life can be a beautiful journey when it is rooted in, through and by LOVE.

If we allow it, our hearts can be hurt by assumptions, lack of understanding, compassion, and grace. But when the opposite is true, the unconditional peace, love and understanding we have for ourselves can grow the deepest roots of long-standing trees.

So we have two choices. Get bitter or get better. Retreat or rebuild. Despise or love. And the answers to these questions? The answers can create a new and healthy awareness of the self-respect we long for.

Be aware of the roots that grow around you. Are they weeds or are they springing life?

Learn from the lessons of loyal love and you'll be amazed at much you will grow.

PICTURE THIS

Have you ever hesitated when something didn't quite sit well with you?

Have you ever changed an answer on a test because you started to doubt your abilities?

Have you ever stayed in a relationship that you knew wasn't what you wanted?

Trust your gut. It's much easier to say than do - but the more you put it into practice, the more loyalty you feel towards yourself.

And the more loyalty you build, the more love you will feel.

Why do we waver or stop ourselves? Why do we change directions or take a turn we didn't intend to take?

Because sometimes we allow that which scares us to direct us, let today be the day the pattern of self-doubt stops – once and for all.

Close your eyes. Picture the best version of yourself and know you are worth the effort.

By focusing on the path to self-respect, you are trusting you are right where you are supposed to be.

You are more than enough – just the way you are.

GIVE UP CONTROL

We can't control what others think or do, but we can control our reactions to them.

Chances are, if someone is operating out of a place of great fear or hate, it is because they have experienced great fear or hate themselves.

It does not excuse their behavior, but it may give us more insights into why they behave how they do.

If someone is not treating you well, it may be time to move on.

Even long-term relationships we engage in can sometimes go from healthy to toxic. And when this happens, it may be time to change your course.

Taking the high road, no matter what the situation, is never easy.

But it is in pursuing self-respect and the path to understanding who we are that allows us to show grace, mercy, and love to ourselves.

Through prayer, acts of kindness, and operating out of a place of forgiveness, we can give up trying to control the outcomes of our lives and let the gift of loyal love truly be found.

DON'T SETTLE

If we allow our insecurities to take over, that's when we tend to settle for less, get into relationships that aren't healthy or look for love in all the wrong places.

Have you been there?

Stop worrying about what other people think.

By focusing on loyal love, you'll gain peace and happiness, and you won't keep worrying about the opinions or thoughts of others.

Chances are a year or 5 years or 10 years now - the people who had the opinions that hurt your heart probably won't even be a part of your life.

Learn how to trust your gut, rely on your instincts and place your worth and value in loving yourself. Be centered through and by beautiful lessons of self-respect along the way.

You are more valuable than the finest riches when you start believing you deserve more.

And you do. Every single day. You deserve more than you can possibly imagine.

NURTURE THE INVESTMENT

We can define who and what is important to us by how we spend our time and what we are willing to juggle to make it all work.

If it's important, we'll find a way. If not, we'll find an excuse.

The same theory applies to taking care of yourself.

You ARE worth the investment.

You deserve a few weekends a year to do what you love. You deserve downtime, quiet time or time to refresh your soul. And yes, you deserve that occasional chocolate croissant.

When we invest in ourselves, we invest in our overall well-being: mind, body and soul.

Let someone else take care of the kids and the pets now and then.

Sign up for the dance class that will challenge you. Walk to the corner and back.

Do something to remind you that YOU are valuable when you practice the art of unconditional self-respect.

Again and again. On good days and bad days and all of the mediocre days in between.

You are loyal love.

GET RID OF THE COVERS

When you're in the midst of all that doesn't make sense, always remember that you're never alone.

Look inside your heart to start knowing the unconditional art of self-respect.

Respecting yourself is a journey worth taking.

When you get to know your heart, you will start to hear a beautiful song.

The lyrics will repeat in your head with a steady rhythm of love, grace, understanding and compassion.

The song will stir your soul to a beautiful place of self-discovery and peace. Through every step of the journey, get to know yourself better than the day before.

On the days you spring out of bed full of energy and on the days when you want to pull the covers over your head and simply lay there, remember when you practice loyal love, you are never alone.

BE A SOURCE OF LIGHT

Do not be afraid.

For fear leads to worry and worry points us down the path to dread.

Do not dread the day.

Instead, find a way to have hope, focus on all that is good in this world, turn away from evil, and know we are not here to please others.

Let us be sources of light shining authentic truth in the deepest recesses of our own hearts.

Choose to walk in self-respect by finding the things that bring you peace.

Do something kind for someone else, expecting nothing in return.

Breathe deeply, meditating on what brings you joy.

We do not live in an ideal world, but through examples of kindness, we can be sources of light.

It's in knowing ourselves that good will overcome evil, one act of loyal love at a time.

FIND TIME TO FORGIVE

It's time to forgive yourself.

It's time to stop blaming the situation and the other person and the circumstances and the addiction and the results of your choices.

It is by and through self-forgiveness that we can take the first steps on the path to complete healing.

No matter what you have faced in the past, remember to focus on the light. Even amid the darkness, know the light will come again.

Extend the same measures of mercy, compassion, understanding and unconditional love to yourself as you do to others.

It may sound easy, but how often do we find ourselves wishing we could redo certain moments? Say things differently? Love more truly?

Don't live in regret but find joy and peace in self-truth.

Let today be a beautiful opportunity for you to quiet your soul, take in personal grace and prepare your hearts for the beautiful, loyal love that is to come.

REMIND YOURSELF WHO YOU ARE

Find confidence from your own loyalty.

What others think or say about you is usually a projection of their own experience or true ignorance about yours.

This is a reminder worth repeating.

When someone tells you what you aren't, show them what you are. What someone tells you that you can't, show them what you can.

Look within the depths of your heart, find out what drives your spirit, and be content in knowing that you are exactly where you should be, as you should be and how you should be.

And the biggest surprise?

You will learn inner confidence through a better understanding of inner peace.

When you let go and make room for reminding yourself who you are, anything is possible.

Be confident in what you are learning from this very moment.

Take heart in knowing that even through the most difficult or challenging lessons in life, you are mastering the art of unconditional self-respect.

RELEASE CONTROL

Instead of grieving for what you don't have, focus on the beautiful and complex layers of everything you are learning and growing from.

This is how you become closer to your goal of loyal love.

Sometimes we are faced with the disappointing actions of people or confusing situations in our lives simply to remind us of exactly what, where, and how we are supposed to be.

Learn to let go and focus on loyal love even if that means loosening your grip on how you thought life was going to unfold.

Once you release control, your heavy stomps will soon feel like you are gliding across the dance floor.

Find the pulse that only your heart will understand and dance like no one is looking. Sometimes you simply have to be willing to learn a few new steps.

The more you trust the music and release control of the rhythm, the more peace, joy and loyal love you will experience within every note of every song.

FIND YOUR VOICE

Be true to your own words and actions. Turn away from fear and embrace the truth of your heart.

Listen to the small steady voice that gives you courage, hope and the innate ability to move towards what you know is right, true and real.

It's not an easy process.

The loud voices of others may drown out your initial whispers a time or two.

But when you finally realize you must stand up for the longings within your heart, when you are open to being led down the path to exactly when, where and how self-respect is supposed to be, your voice will rise above the noise of the world.

As your lyrical melody abounds, you will begin to trust your journey. And even when you agree to disagree with those you love or as people come in and out of your life, remember this: no one else can live out your personal story.

It's in finding the serenity to accept the things you cannot change, courage to change the things you can, and wisdom to know the difference – loyal love is yours.

Be clear. Stay focused. And let your voice be heard.

CHANGE YOUR INNER VOICE

Approach each day with hope.

Remember that misery is only an option. You can choose to celebrate even in the midst of challenging times.

An attitude of unconditional self-respect is a decision.

Everyone has problems. Everyone has areas in their lives that don't make sense.

Often, we can't change our circumstance. But we can change our attitude towards them. We always have a choice.

When you have a bad attitude, you're usually going to point out what's wrong about every situation.

When you have a positive attitude, even if you must crawl out of your cave of darkness, you can find something positive to say and do.

So today, on this beautiful day of loyal love, you can actively choose to love yourself in and through the journey. Be an advocate of self-respect instead of a victim of feeling sorry for yourself.

You're alive. You're you. And that is more than enough.

SHOW YOUR COMPASSION

The importance of compassion, understanding and kindness can be our daily response and our first reaction.

Our ability to welcome, care and support one another, even on the days that are simply designed to teach life's lessons, is a priceless and everlasting gift.

Showing grace and mercy through an encouraging word, a listening ear, or refusing to immerse ourselves in gossip, is a journey that doesn't come with a detailed map.

If we remember that everyone is going through something, our defenses will drop, and we'll begin to look up and out instead of within a circle of exclusivity.

Our example can be powerful if we are open and true to what we say and how we engage with those we encounter along our journeys.

You can choose to honor each person's travels through life, even when their path is vastly different than your own.

As you dedicate yourself to loyal love – show kindness to your own heart.

As your heart opens, so will your mind. Continue to write your story - one beautiful word of compassion at a time.

HONOR YOUR BEING

Be the type of person who will drop everything just to listen to someone else's heart.

Be the type of person who doesn't put pressure on yourself or others.

Be the type of person who never underestimates your abilities, talents or potential.

Be the type of person who always wants to learn more without sounding like they already know what life is teaching them.

Be the type of person who wants to work through the tough times and who truly wants to understand the viewpoints and opinions of others.

Be the type of person who will steadfastly point out the good and who will focus on the very joy of this day, a day of loyal love.

Be the type of person who lets their actions speak louder than words - no matter the situation or circumstance.

Be the type of person who can look at themselves in the mirror and know they did their best, had fun and gave themselves grace.

Be the type of person who can hear your heart song when the room is silent and who can find something to celebrate every day.

Be EXACTLY the type of person you were always meant to be.

STRIVE TOWARDS HOPE

In the depths of your disappointments, there is hope. In the darkest corners of your pain, there is mercy. In the tears that flow down your face, there is a deeper understanding of your heart.

We all have a story behind the sparkle in our eyes, the wrinkles on our face and the scars of our soul.

Every day we can strive to be the best version of ourselves we know how to be - rooted in unconditional respect, grace and kindness that knows no boundaries.

Attempt to take the high road, be gentle with yourself and your tender spirit, and always remember, even on the days when your world feels like it has been turned upside down; you can choose to react out of love.

Hold close to those you trust. Keep your heart open and your mind aware. When life throws you a few curveballs, make the most of every at-bat. Success will come in learning from your failures and adjusting as you go.

Ask for support as you need it or even before you reach that point. Never stop believing that there is goodness in each person, even when it's difficult to see at times.

DO NOT GROW WEARY

Do not grow weary or heavyhearted. Embrace the lessons of the journey. For when you least expect it, goodness will come.

Goodness will come.

Even when others may try to intimidate you or build themselves up by putting you down, you can make a choice.   On the days when the behaviors and words of those you interact with don't make any sense, you can still choose happy.

Decide, right here and now, to turn away from bitterness and pain. Focus on what you have learned, the strength you have gained, and the ability to listen to that small steady voice, knowing all the while, it will not misguide you.

Your instincts are powerful, poignant, and if we are honest with ourselves, they are usually telling us exactly what we need to hear, believe and accept.

So as the sun sets on another day and the anticipation of morning draws near, be aware of each emotion you are having.

It's when we can LISTEN to what is in the depths of our heart and the whisperings of our soul, that it is far easier to get back on the path of self-respect, one thoughtful reaction at a time.

FIND THE STEPPING STONES

The journey to self-respect is paved by the stepping stones of your experiences. Everything you go through brings you further along your path.

Some steps will be more painful than others. Some steps will leave you feeling sucker punched and scratching your head, wondering what happened to a friendship or relationship you were once so sure of at one point in time.

Other steps will point you in a completely different direction than you anticipated - away from judgment, closemindedness and toxicity.

Don't be afraid of a path towards new beginnings. Embrace the hope of loyal love and start seeing self-respect as a gift of joy, driven by a new sense of purpose.

Remember this: mixed among the stones of your path are also beautiful cobblestones of unconditional love, hope, encouragement and peace that surpasses ALL understanding.

You are not a sum of your past mistakes, nor should you allow others to treat you based upon them. The lessons in life make your heart, mind and soul stronger, bolder and truer.

Keep on walking. Share your authenticity from the depths of your soul. And never be afraid to express exactly who you are, what you stand for and what makes you - YOU.

ACT ON MERCY

When is the last time you showed a little mercy and compassion towards yourself?

Before your feet hit the floor, remind yourself that you are enough.

Focus on taking in the goodness of the day and let go of the rest. In each deep and cleansing breath, let your journey to self-respect gently remind you to cast your cares and to keep your eyes focused on loyal love.

In all things, both seen and unseen. Through all you don't understand. Through what is designed to teach you life's lessons. Through what you are passionate about. And everything else in between.

In those few moments, let the peace in your heart stop the worry of your mind. Let the joy of your spirit gently brush away rumblings of complaining or frustration.

Today is a new day.

A day filled with loyal love.

Show mercy towards others as well as yourself.

Stay positive.

Be grateful.

And begin again.

IT'S GOING TO BE OK

Have you ever had a day or two or ten when you feel like life isn't moving forward, but only going around in circles?

In a society that is results driven, sometimes putting one foot in front of the other can be more overwhelming than others possibly know.

On those days, it's good to remember you are doing the best you can. It's more than OK to be who you are, without judgment, criticism or comparison. On some days, simply waking up, stretching and breathing are enough.

Other mornings, it's OK to stay under the covers for a few extra minutes., let the tears fall down your face, and do what you need to do for yourself, your family or your circumstances.

Maybe the circles of life are more about the journey of self-respect than our destination. When we let go of expectations that weigh us down, something amazing happens: we are free to simply be our unique, real, authentic selves.

It's in that authentic truth that loyal love blossoms.

When we learn to unconditionally love ourselves for who we are, we can take in the goodness of each day and dare to find our heart's longing. Not overnight, but one beautiful moment at a time.

SURPASS YOUR POTENTIAL

Never limit your dreams because of fear of the unknown.

If you can imagine the potential for what will be, you have already started your journey towards reaching your new summit.

When you come to the end of all that is familiar, the journey of self-respect will meet you on your path and gently direct your steps, however gingerly they need to be taken.

So on this day, a day of loyal love, challenge yourself out of your normal comfort zone.

Believe that you can. Dream that you will. Imagine the life that will bring you a peace that surpasses all understanding. Will the timing always line up for how you originally thought it would? Probably not.

But know the mastery of the marathon is far better than the surface of any sprint.

Listen to your heart. Connect with a mentor. Grab a friend for a cup of coffee. Vent!

Instead of focusing on your limitations, know that you can achieve the musings of your soul.

Simply trust that small steady voice guiding your heart. Say "yes" to knowing that even when the road is unclear, there is a new and beautiful path awaiting you, one small step of self-respect at a time.

TAKE TIME TO LISTEN

Are you listening?

Do you pay attention to that still small voice that whispers to you from the depths of your soul?

Are you listening?

Do you ignore what your mind knows and what your heart has yet to accept?

Are you listening?

In a world that is hurried and without pause, take the time to clear your head, get silent despite everything around you and simply: LISTEN.

L: Love yourself enough to know when it's time to walk away.
I: Ignite your passions by making room for them in your soul.
S: Stand strong in realizing how you deserve to be treated.
T: Teach love, kindness and respect in all you do and say.
E: Enjoy the journey and learn from every challenge.
N: Notice when you need a break from the ongoing noise.

On this day of loyal love, take the time to listen. Instead of focusing on what you are going to say next or how you are going to solve someone else's problem, immerse yourself in sweet silence. Breathe deeply, honor the quiet and know that the power of listening is giving you more strength for your journey than words ever can.

DON'T LET THE GHOSTS HAUNT YOU

People come into your life for a season, reason or a lifetime.

If someone decides to exit your life - stops talking, calling, texting, emailing or any other mode of communication, it says volumes about their character, integrity and courage.

Actually, it says volumes about their LACK of character, integrity and courage.

If you are in the midst of a confusing season, know any pain you feel now will help you fully heal later.

Sometimes it's beyond challenging to let go of those we thought we knew or shared a portion of our life with.   Sometimes the tears will give way to anger and anger to sadness and sadness to loss.

It's OK to let go now.   Don't let the ghosts of your past affect your present. You are far too valuable to let what or who lurks in the dark ruin your light.

Run through the haunted house and come out smiling.   Look at yourself in the mirror and know you are stronger than the demons who once crossed your path.

Be free.

GO THROUGH

You cannot control the behaviors, thoughts, and actions of another, but you can control your reactions to them." ~ Joyce Meyer

Allow yourself to know most people are simply trying to do the best they can, as they are, and as life comes. Authentically flawed and beautifully human - during the good days and the bad – everyone is going through.

Realize our paths are ever changing. Make mistakes and learn from those mistakes. When we know better, we do better. Don't judge; listen. Don't cast the first stone, but instead offer to help.

Every person you know is going through something - living out their own stories, at a pace that is right for them.

As we move forward - without a magic wand to heal those battling horrible health issues, or to give peace to those whom are struggling with relationships or to instill confidence in those who have lost their hope- let go and find your loyal love.

When your heart overflows with compassion but everything is still spinning around you, treat yourself and others with grace, kindness, forgiveness and gentleness.

Go through and not around. Know it's ok to be tired, rest, and regroup. When we simply realize the fragility of our souls, we can enter the path to self-respect.

KNOW THE REAL YOU

There are those who know what you do for your job, sport or hobby.

But only you can understand how and why your disappointments, passions, challenges and successes drive you.

There are those who know where you were born or where you grew up.

But only you can understand how your former fears and insecurities tend to shape your words and actions. If you don't prepare yourself mentally, emotionally and spiritually, you can quickly forget the longings of your soul.

Why let those who know the surface parts about you think they understand the depths of what makes you – you.

At every stage of your journey, take the time to get to know the real you.

The path to self-respect is about fully acknowledging, accepting and immersing yourself in the complexities of your mind, heart and soul.

Be thankful for those who know you, but also remember to cherish the person who understands you the most – all you have to do is look in the mirror to find them.

RESPECT YOURSELF

The journey to self-respect can be painful if it is rushed, non-authentic or noisy.

The more you turn away from the situations or people who are not healthy, the more you will discover your true center of peace.

As you realize who you are and what you are meant for in this world, the first step to wholeness is what Aretha Franklin so beautifully sang about: RESPECT.

The more you respect your inner voice, the more loyal love you will feel. And the more peace in your heart, the easier it is to move forward to a place of truth.

So how do you start the journey to respect? By breaking it down.

Realize you are more than enough.

Exhale when life gets overwhelming.

Start carving out time to do what you love.

Point out the positive in yourself every day.

Expect good things and good things will follow.

Cherish the simple gift of each day.

Trust your gut.

GET REAL

Sometimes the greatest rewards can be found in the simplest of circles. At the heart of communication is the circle made up of equal parts- both sharing and listening.

When you take the time to open up and get real, when you share your thoughts and opinions, it's amazing how much you can learn about what makes you – you.

Stop closing yourself off and living life on the surface.

Go deeper. Be vulnerable. And when you ask someone how they are doing, wait for more than a one-word answer.

As the saying goes, people are often fighting battles you know nothing about. Why? Because we often get too inward focused to notice.

Remind yourself that investing a listening ear and an open non-judgmental heart is the best way to truly learn about compassion, forgiveness and grace.

So on this day of loyal love, take a deep breath, listen from your heart and when the time is right, respond with kindness, mercy and unconditional love.

DON'T GIVE UP

None of us are here by accident, but somewhere amid the incredible chaos of our daily routine, we sometimes forget about the good we can do.

When we practice the art of loyal love, our humanity can bring peace instead of turmoil.

When we start to understand the beauty of self-respect, our hearts can extend love rather than indifference.

When we accept who we are and what makes us the individual we are, our minds can solve problems rather than create them.

And when our souls can exude compassion, we will gain understanding and grace that knows no boundaries.

Don't give up – move forward. Let today be a beautiful illustration of loyal love and self-respect.

Now is the time to start being good to yourself. The only way our broken world can be fixed is by not showing this goodness – first to ourselves and then to others.

Give it a try. And see what a life-changing difference you can make.

BE JUST THE WAY YOU ARE

You are amazing just the way you are.

At this moment, reading these words, let your heart not be hardened by disappointments, but be open to all that is good, be ready for what is waiting for you right around the corner.

Truly, even when people let you down or behave in ways that are difficult to understand, you have the awesome power to let it all go.

And in the letting go, there is a truly beautiful world just waiting to be discovered: one of hope, happiness, love, peace and joy.

Believe the best. Always.

Do not pass judgment on someone else or close yourself off after you are hurt. Rather, learn from the disappointments. Simply stop to remember everyone is a work in progress.

Everyone has a story, and even if you came along someone's side and helped them through their darkest or most vulnerable hour, that is no guarantee they will return the favor.

Stop being disappointed in the world and start finding happiness within your own soul of loyal love.

DON'T WASTE A MOMENT

Circumstances change.

Some are for the better and some are inexplicable.

How one person handles themselves through stress or trial can also make the person you once knew, unrecognizable.

Remember to stay true to your heart. How someone else defines their journey is only theirs alone.

So when you have a low day or when the hurts you are feeling make you start to lose hope, try this: stop, regroup and find your center.

Close your eyes, breathe in all that is good, and release everything which boggles the mind.

Know how easy it is to forget to practice what we preach - letting go and moving forward takes time.

While some relationships are unconditional, some are only seasonal, designed to teach you about who you are, what you deserve and what you believe in the depths of your heart.

You have the unique ability to surround yourself with goodness and walk away from what doesn't fill your soul. That task is yours, and some days are going to be better than others.

No one else can possibly understand what you have been through, or why you react out of the emotion you do.

Don't waste a moment trying to explain yourself. Let this day of loyal love teach you to keep being you.

ACKNOWLEDGE THE WEAKNESS

Acknowledging our hidden weaknesses can turn into newly discovered strengths. Understanding our vulnerabilities can be our most authentic sources of loyal love truth.

When we lose our way, we start paying attention to the compass within our hearts and the gentle rhythm that creates a new song.

For every hurt, disappointment or heartbreak, the cracks in our armor are not designed to make us feel like we have lost the battle - instead the breaks are there to let the light shine through.

If you are wrestling with all you can't possibly understand, get ready. The journey of self-respect is teaching you exactly what you value, love and cherish.

And maybe, just maybe, the tears rolling down your face and keeping you up at night, will remind you of this:

It is in the emptiest of moments our hearts, minds and souls are being restored and renewed.

Do not lose hope.

A brand-new chapter is about to be written.

CHOOSE LOVE

In a world that feels like it is upside down and sideways, it's understandable to be weary, downtrodden, and even cynical.

Our spirits are tired. Our souls feel weak. Our minds are burdened as we look for a glimmer of light at the end of this dark tunnel.

We can sit and question how and why our world is filled with hate, intolerance and tragedy.

Or we can brush ourselves off, stand up and DO something.

In reality, these acts are happening all around us, but they are rarely broadcast on the news.

So, what should you do?

Choose happiness.
Be kind.
Focus on the good.
Give instead of receive.
Extend a smile.
Organize a gathering of old friends.
Meet new people.
Surround yourself with those who aren't the same as you are, even when it means getting out of your comfort zone to do so.

Through the smallest acts of kindness, grace, mercy and understanding, we can show love to ourselves by choosing acts of love, no matter what.

ADJUST AS YOU GO

We all do the best we can, make mistakes, try what works and learn from what doesn't.

And we adjust. Again and again and again.

Learning the art of unconditional self-respect is as much about the lessons learned as it is about the journey.

Amid each and every circumstance, learn to stand up for what you believe in, not against something else.

Always give and show mercy and grace every day.

Not only to others, but to yourself.

Not only in your words, but in your actions.

When we are passionate about what ignites our hearts, sometimes we forget a simple truth: the path that is right for one person is not always the same path that is right for someone else.

If you start with a basic understanding that life is designed to teach and not to harm, to love and not to hate, and to find hope and not despair then somehow making adjustments towards loyal love gets a little bit easier – one simple act of self-respect at a time.

BREAK OUT OF YOUR COCOON

Taking an honest look into your own heart is the foundation of self-respect.

Courage is necessary, not just for the times when life is filled with simple routine, but through the days when memories of your past attempt to hit pause on your future.

If you are ignored, ghosted, dismissed, told you are crazy, or made to feel like you have done something wrong for simply standing up for yourself, keep standing.

Never stop going through. A caterpillar doesn't become a butterfly in one day.

Always listen to your inner voice, however small and steady it may be. Live out what is in your heart. Even when your journey takes a few unexpected twists and turns, remember it is a series of simple steps which will guide you to where you are supposed to be.

Be open to reading the internal signs and following your personal GPS. And on the tough days when the words and actions of others don't make sense, keep being authentic to what you say and how you say it.

Wings of bravery and self-worth sometimes take years to develop. The time is now to wake up, break out of your cocoon and fly.

EXTEND ABUNDANT BLESSINGS

Abundant blessings are often found during our weakest moments.

Owning up to what makes us human and admitting our vulnerabilities instead of creating an illusion of self-righteous perfection is one of the most important parts of our journey towards the path of loyal love.

If we are honest, finding blessings in each day can be more challenging when we are comparing our lives to someone else's journey.

While we are told to focus on what we are grateful for, there is also the reality that waves of comparison tend to hit out of nowhere – when planning vacations, buying a car, choosing a school, playing a sport or working on our yard.

Stop trying to measure the success of your days to what you see. Instead, forge the path to self-respect by allowing yourself to understand your own voice.

As you count your blessings throughout the coming days, challenge yourself to get real instead of perfect. You are a blessing simply by being you.

Let loyal love be the foundation of your words and actions. Extend an extra measure of grace, love, and support to those who are hurting – even when that person is you.

LOOK AHEAD

Stop looking behind you.

What's done is done. Instead, learn from the lesson. None of us are perfect. We are all trying the best we can. When we know better, we try to do better.

People change.

The person you once held a sacred spot for in your heart may have walked away without warning or treated you without respect or love.

Repeat this phrase every single day until it is a part of your DNA:

I cannot control the words and behaviors of other people. I can only control my reactions to them.

Got it? Try it again.

I cannot control the words and behaviors of other people. I can only control my reactions to them.

Hurt. Anger. Frustration. Disappointment. Let yourself be present in every emotion – even if when they are all hitting you at once.

And then, no matter how many tears flow down your face, remember the beauty of unconditionally loving, respecting and nurturing your tender heart, mind and soul.

It'll sting for a while. But then one day, you'll wake up KNOWING you deserve better. You deserve unconditional loyal love - not from others, but from the simple act of loving and accepting yourself throughout this beautiful journey called life.

WALK THE WALK

Loyal love is about being an example of talking the talk and walking the walk.

Self-respect is about knowing that after every storm, there is always a rainbow of hope waiting to shine through and illuminate our broken world with rays of glorious light.

In this very moment, this teachable moment, and in the days, weeks, months, and years to come, it is time to remind ourselves and our children about the importance of kindness, self-respect, inclusion, and unconditional loyal love.

As we each walk along our journeys, there is much our hearts and minds cannot comprehend. But know this: there are opportunities - every single day - to turn our backs on hate, bullying, and injustice by loving ourselves and nurturing our souls.

The next time you start to put someone down for whatever makes them slightly different than you are - stop and remember they may be struggling with their own journey of loyal love.

Reach out to those who are hurting, vulnerable or hungry. Pick up the phone to check in on a friend or someone you haven't seen eye to eye with in the past. Hold a door, share a smile, and let love win.

Get to know yourself by listening more and talking less. Before you retort out of anger, pause. You'll be amazed by the common ground we can find when loyal love is our foundation.

EXPECT SOMETHING GREAT

Instead of waiting for the other shoe to drop out of dread or fear, expect something good to happen to you.

Go on. Dare to believe things will get better. It all starts with how you approach it.

Even on your darkest days, don't go around the hurt, frustration or sadness. Embrace where you are, as you are and who you are. KNOW that even when the shoe does indeed drop, you will have the strength, resilience and trust that you need because of your foundation of loyal love.

Even when you don't understand the situation you are going through, you will always be ok.

If you don't want to turn the page quite yet, lean into the next few paragraphs of your life. Stop concerning yourself with what others think and instead find peace in realizing that through the ups and downs of life, through the successes and disappointments, the only person who can live your life is YOU.

Self-respect is also a journey of faith.

You may feel like you are feeling your way through the dark, but you can actually see the light at the end of the tunnel when you decide to look for it. The more you TRUST who you are, flaws included, the more you will learn, grow and be happy.

LIVE YOUR STORY

Be the person your journey of self-respect has made you to be.

Nothing more. Nothing less. Know that your passions, interests, fears, dreams and what ultimately defines you is completely unique to you alone.

What makes you laugh, what makes you cry, and what you hold dear is an ever-changing story: YOUR story.

Each one of us have different experiences that shape who we are, the decisions we make, and what our futures will hold. Today is an opportunity to learn more.

Embrace the pages of your story, and when you need to, reread a chapter or two. There's nothing wrong with repeating a lesson until you can accept it as your own.

Truly, even in the most challenging of circumstances, loyal love is within you. The path you have chosen is designed to teach you something amazing and give you a wonderful opportunity to be an even better person that you were the day before.

So as today unfolds and a world of possibilities with it, turn away from judgment and embrace more loyal love.

GIVE POWER TO THE FUTURE

Ghosting is cruel.

Ghosting is selfish.

Ghosting is all about someone else's deepest insecurities, fears and mistrusts.

When a relationship ends, it can hurt. But when a relationship ends without so much as a word - when someone stops all communication - the darkness can feel like it is never going to turn into light.

It's ok to mourn when someone you once held dear to your heart suddenly vanishes from your life.

If you have the opportunity to make things right, do it.

If you have the chance to explain to someone what is hurting or what has offended you, go ahead and explain it.

But if you never hear a word back in return?

Remember this:

When you purposely inflict pain on someone else's heart, there's nothing beneficial in that. But when you pick up the pieces of that pain, turn the page and keep moving forward, the ghosts no longer have any power over any part of you.

You can and will find strength in moving on. You will get through. And even in the awkward moments, you will find peace in letting go and allowing the journey of self-respect to set you free.

MEET THE PEOPLE OF YOUR TO BE

Your friends will change as you do.

Stop holding on to your past relationships. The more you hold on to what was - the less opportunity you will have to meet the people of your to be.

Will it hurt your heart when a friend decides your relationship is over before you do? Yes. Letting go is a process, especially if you have known that person for half a lifetime.

But your heart will be filled with happiness, peace and joy after realizing how far you've come, what you've learned from those friendships and what you deserve.

Remember, the words and actions of others do not reflect you who are. If someone walks away, shuts you out or goes dark, close that door and know there is a window of new relationships simply waiting for you to find them.

Each day can be filled with loyal love when we start to understand our journey of self-respect is a marathon and not a sprint.

Form a new circle with people who love you where, how and just as you are.

NO MATTER THE SEASON

Always assume that everybody is going through something - what they share and what they hold close to the vest.

No matter the season of life, remember it is in respecting our differences and acknowledging our need to be heard that we can continue to know ourselves and what makes us unique.

Truly, we ALL have the potential to be a positive part of humanity and its great capacity for unconditional loyal love.

Do the best you can, keep it real, and embrace the imperfect mess you are. The funny part? The more you accept who you are, the happier every season of your life will be.

Find thanksgiving in knowing that through your missteps, you also can journey towards an even greater path than the one you were originally walking upon.

No matter the season of life, may you experience the joy of acceptance, grace, and love that will fill your heart, mind, and spirit with the goodness of humanity, the lessons of self-worth and all its beautiful blessings.

TRUST THE REAL YOU

During an age where we are digitally connected, we are also sometimes emotionally disconnected from our most important relationships.

Why are we so hard on ourselves instead of honoring who we are as works in progress?

Why do we lash out at others instead of giving the same kindness we so desperately need to show ourselves?

Why do we let disappointments become a mental barrier to our future? Because somewhere along the way, the number of likes or followers started to define our self-worth.

And you know what? That's not ok.

Instead, every day, we should get up, do the best we can, and know the progress we make today will help set the stage for a better tomorrow.

Once you learn to accept yourself unconditionally, flaws and all, you will truly start connecting to your own heart again.

And once you connect to what is true, you will have a better grasp on how to make peace with who you are at this very moment. Stop worrying about your image or the social media version of your life. Instead, focus on the smiles, tears, joys, frustrations, fears and passions that make you - YOU.

CONNECT AND BE FREE

The beauty of the human spirit is its ability to connect, through word, thought and action.

Each morning we rise, we have the wonderful opportunity to choose if we are going to connect with the world we live in and get in sync with our own heartbeat or build a fortress around our hearts that does not let us be who we are meant to be.

No matter what cards life has dealt us, we can find our voice and compassion through understanding our spirit, opening ourselves up and embracing the vulnerability that comes in sharing who we are and what is in our hearts.

By being honest with those we love, no matter how difficult the subject, we connect through pure honesty. People are put along our path for a reason. If we choose another route to avoid the encounter, then we also lose the ability to learn from that person.

Keep pushing beyond your limits. Explore your passion, find your voice and learn from those around you. Pick up the phone. Send an email. Schedule a coffee date with someone who's been on your heart. Clear up a misunderstanding. Push yourself out of your comfort zone and embrace the goodness, light, peace, and joy that is available to you.

As a new day approaches, connect to your journey of self-respect and be free.

BE PRESENT

Why do we tend to run towards what our heart knows isn't healthy for us?

Why do we sometimes walk away from the people who love us the most?

Because sometimes the people who love us the most tell us the things we don't want to hear: the truth.

As you have journeyed through learning the art of unconditional self-respect, the importance of being in the present moment is key to understanding the truth about ourselves.

No matter what mistakes you have made in your past, even if some of those mistakes were repeated, don't look back any longer.

The less time you spend worrying about the future or what other people think about you, the healthier you will be.

Focus on your confidence. This is only possible when you accept everything about your character - the good, the bad and yes, even the ugly.

The more you understand what makes you the beautiful human being you are, the more you will follow the path to loyal love - one meaningful step at a time.

SUSTAIN YOUR CHARACTER

Dysfunction stems from a lack of confidence. Whether emotional, physical, mental or spiritual, the more kindness, grace and mercy we show to ourselves, the healthier our lives will become.

It is impossible to grow and eventually sustain your character with faulty confidence. The more you learn to love who you are at this very moment, the more your confidence will be built

Sometimes it's okay to be glad about the rejection because through the rejection you found a strength you never knew you had.

Dr. Seuss once wrote, "Don't cry because it's over, smile because it happened." His approach to his writing and his life was consistently built around this theme.

So today, on this day of loyal love, sustain your character by finding something to smile about. Even if that same situation once made you sob into your pillow at night - close your eyes, take a deep breath and be grateful for the lesson.

After all, you may not be where you thought you'd be, but chances are, you are wiser, stronger and more confident from the journey.

PUSH THE LIMITS

Each day we rise, we are given a beautiful new opportunity to explore, dare and dream.

Today, there is a fresh canvas just waiting for us to splash some paint on it. We may not know what the full picture looks like, but creating art is all about our imagination.

And our imaginations are limitless.

Pushing past the boundaries we set for ourselves is often a difficult task. Trying new things is intimidating, but once you trust your natural instincts and go for it, the rewards are worth far more than your fears.

Why not challenge yourself with something you have never done before?

The worse thing that can happen? You'll gain experience, courage and determination.

So on this day of self-respect, explore what is in your soul, dare to push your limits and dream with a heart full of joy, hope and unconditional loyal love.

Loyal Love

NEVERTHELESS, LET IT UNFOLD

Give it time.

A good reminder during any season of joyful expectation but unanswered questions.

Even when you don't understand the why, when or how, your heart is up to something good. How do you trust the steps of your journey when they take you to a different path than you originally anticipated? How do you know it will all work out, even when challenges, setbacks or hurdles slow down your journey?

By trusting your faith. Faith is not the absence of doubt. It's the willingness to stand by and through ALL you can't see, feel or explain.

It's never too late to begin again. As a new season in your life begins to unfold, consider learning the art of unconditional self-respect.

You've already started by reading this book. So, keep going!

Be intentionally thoughtful and kinder to yourself today than you were yesterday. Do not beat yourself up or put pressure on yourself when things don't go the way you thought they would.

Reset. And fill your mind, body and spirit with loyal love, self-respect and compassion.

Have fun, do your best and know the journey of becoming who you were meant to be starts and ends with you.

STAY THE COURSE

The beautiful journey of life is designed to teach, redirect and give us pause.

And on the days where the pause feels like an unanswered prayer?

Embrace the poignant moments. Give yourself the freedom to gain amazing insights that change as you do. Don't just seek encouragement, be an encourager. Reach out, both to and for one another.

Pay attention to your quilt pieces. The ones that keep you warm through steadfast prayer, patience and an understanding that can only come from simple acts of grace, forgiveness and unconditional loyal love.

Be encouraged. Keep a positive perspective. Do not fear. Walk in self-respect.

And know that the path ahead, although filled with many twists and turns, is truly a meaningful and unique journey.

When we know better, we do better. So on this day of loyal love, remember to stay the course. No matter what you are facing, go out and make a difference, one brilliant step at a time.

YOU ARE MORE THAN ENOUGH

There is no one else just like you. So why do we drive ourselves crazy trying to be just like everyone else?

Try this exercise. Repeat after me.

"I am more than enough."

"I am learning how to love me as me."

When we change for the better, we open ourselves up to the lessons. Get rid of what weighs you down. Just because someone looks like they have everything together on the outside doesn't mean they actually do.

The road to comparison brings nothing but havoc, disappointment and envy.

But the journey to self-love, respect and worth? That is a path filled with light, peace and grace. Stop worrying about what you lack and embrace the gifts you do have.

You are more than enough. And you can learn to love yourself with a loyal and unconditional love - one moment at a time.

SLOW THE SPINNING TOP

Have you ever watched a spinning toy? If you spin it hard enough, or with enough force, it will go round and round in a perfect spiral.

You can get mesmerized by watching the top spin. But eventually, as the spinning stops, the top begins to wobble and slowly but surely, the spinning top will fall in one side, and come to rest, worn and off balance.

In today's fast paced society, we often keep our lives in spinning top mode. If we spin hard enough and with enough force, we will keep spinning and spinning until our days are one blurred mess.

Things get off for a variety of reasons.

Health. Hormones. Disagreements. Agreements. Work. The human condition.

Spinning tops. Spinning tops. Spinning tops that get wobbly and when they finally start to slow down, fall over to one side.

How do you stop the spinning? By slowing down.

Will you feel a bit dizzy for a while? Probably. But once you truly allow yourself to slow down, you will then see the beauty of each color, pattern and texture – the art of being you.

LOOK AT YOU!

Have you ever looked back on a situation in your life and wondered, "What the heck was I thinking?"

Have you ever run into someone you dated, years later, and thought, "Were they always so unkind and self-centered?"

Every person that crosses your path is supposed to intersect with where you are at that given moment. And when the moment is over, whether 11 months, 11 years, or a lifetime later, you will find yourself pondering these moments in time and all they were designed to teach you.

You know what?

You have come so very far.   And here is why.

Through every tear of hurt, you let go of exactly how you didn't want to be treated. Every time you took time out just for you, you honored your heart and taught it to heal. Each time you took the high road, you ventured further down the path to self-respect.

And even if you aren't quite where you want to be sure yet, you should celebrate how far you have come. Your life may look wildly different than what you thought it was going to look like.   But your journey is your own.

Walk on, sweet friend. With your head held a bit higher, with your shoulders back and with the confidence of knowing the journey to loyal love, learning the art of unconditional self-respect begins and ends with you.

WHAT WE KNOW NOW

What is that saying? When we know better, we do better.

Believe it or not, you know better today than you did yesterday.

During our teenage years and even through our 20s and 30s, it's tough to remember or even comprehend the meaning of loyal self-respect.

In our younger years, we may have put our value in the hands of other people. The guy (or girl) we were dating. The grade we earned on a test. How many points we scored on the basketball court. How much money we make. Or the number on the scale.

NONE of these things should have had power over our self-respect, but without the experience of life, they sometimes do.

What we learn through every relationship, exam, game, job or diet is this: self-worth starts by learning to love yourself. Not just love yourself, but LOYALLY love yourself.

That takes times. It takes trial and error. It takes situations that you simply must go through and not around. It takes owning up to your mistakes, learning from them and moving on.

It takes more strength than you ever knew you were capable of - and it takes deciding, once and for all, that you are worth it.

PAY ATTENTION

When we pay attention to how we spend our time, who we spend it with and when we feel heard, valued and loved, we are moving closer to unconditional self-respect.

Understanding what is in the deep recesses of our hearts will be reflected not only in how we treat others but how we allow ourselves to be treated.

No matter our circumstances or theirs, we can fully begin to experience our journey to joy.

Hold your head up, say a prayer for your soul to be healed and know that for every friendship you have lost, there is an even greater one waiting to be found.

When you learn to loyally love yourself, your friendships will be consistent, honest and unconditional.

Not just when it's convenient for the other person, but when it's healthy from both sides.

Mutual respect. Authentic grace. Deep understanding. Loyal love attributes that we can learn by focusing on self-respect one situation at a time.

SET YOURSELF FREE

Everyone has a story.

But when the people in your life don't listen to your current chapter, it's ok to take a break.

If you are only giving grace and not receiving any in return, it's more than necessary to give your heart some space.

When others lack the compassion to understand your words, that's when it's time to start walking down a new path.

Learn the art of unconditional self-respect by loyally loving who you are and what you stand for.

Before you know it, you'll discover the boundaries you set are actually making you more free.

MAKE SOME ROOM

Breathe in. Breathe out. Repeat.

No one ever said the journey to unconditional self-respect was going to be an easy one.

Those tears you have wiped away when a certain page hit your square between the eyes?   That's the power of our human connection.

You are not alone, sweet friend. There is great power in personally deciding what your circle looks like.

And you know what?   Your circle is going to change.   Sure, there will be lifelong friends and family and co-workers, but people change, families change and jobs change.

That's a good thing.

When you let go of the people who don't want to be in your life, you make room for the people who do.

It's time to make some room, don't you think?

Clear your mind, open your heart and respect yourself enough to completely walk away from the people or situations that are not good for you.

At the end of the day, that's all **Loyal Love: Learning the Art of Unconditional Self-Respect** is about: making room for what brings you peace and honoring your heart, mind and soul through every moment of your journey.

57159265R00081

Made in the USA
Columbia, SC
06 May 2019